A BANDERSNATCH
DISCUSSION GUIDE

A BANDERSNATCH DISCUSSION GUIDE

Questions and Suggestions for Readers, Writers, Creatives, and Collaborators

Based on *BANDERSNATCH* by Diana Pavlac Glyer

By Roslynn Pryor and Tonia Hurst
Illustrations by James A. Owen
Introduction by Diana Pavlac Glyer

Lindale & Assoc.
A division of TreeHouseStudios

ISBN-13: 978-1-937283-06-3

FIRST EDITION 2019
Printed in the United States of America

To J. R. R. Tolkien. In December 1929, you trembled as you handed the rough draft of "The Lay of Leithian" to your friend C. S. Lewis and asked him if he might like to read it. All of this, all of it, was made possible by that impossible act of raw courage. We are forever in your debt.

Contents

Introduction

Writers need each other. Creativity thrives in community. Those two ideas are the foundation for everything I write about C. S. Lewis, J. R. R. Tolkien, and their writing group, the Inklings. I am appalled that the Myth of the Solitary Genius has robbed generations of writers from the joy of having their creative vision sustained by the encouragement, praise, correction, inspiration, help, and support of others. As Gertrude Stein asserted, "Whenever you write a book, you need someone to say yes to it."

That is the heartbeat of my book Bandersnatch: The Creative Collaboration of C. S. Lewis, J. R. R. Tolkien, and the Inklings. It has been a joy to see writers and scholars discover that the Inklings are wonderful role models of what successful collaboration looks like. Not only did the Inklings collaborate well, they also sustained it for nearly two decades. We do well to learn from their example.

Each of my books has been produced in collaboration, and this Discussion Guide is no exception. It was developed in the context of a highly collaborative project: my work with Michael Ward, Michael Lee, and others to produce an audiobook of Bandersnatch. This Discussion Guide was designed to add value to that inspired project.

Since then, this Discussion Guide has been enjoyed by many readers. It has been used in writing groups, art schools, book clubs, and English classes. It has sustained collaborations that have launched businesses, started ministries, created Writing Centers, directed conferences, and enriched those who create poems, novels, screenplays, graphic novels, songs, videos, workshops, paintings, and other projects that are, in fact, nothing less than the work of their heart.

I can hardly express how grateful I am to Roslynn and Tonia for bringing their unique perspective to this ongoing project. They are skilled teachers: they bring the grit and honesty of those who know how to bring a subject alive in the classroom.

I believe this Guide will continue to be of enormous help to anyone to wants to dive deep into the inner workings of the Inklings in order to discover what the Inklings have to say to us today. Students will find it useful in the classroom; Book Clubs will find it a faithful guide to getting the most of out their reading; writers and artists will thrive as these questions push them to reflect and go deeper; writing groups will explore the depth and breadth of what their ongoing connection has to offer.

A word for those who want to find a writing group and don't know where to start: start here. Find one other person, just one, and invite them to read Bandersnatch with you and work through the questions here in this Guide. The rest of the process will unfold before your eyes.

Remembering, as Charles Williams declared, "We are necessary to each other."

Diana Pavlac Glyer
Glendora, California

READ THIS FIRST:

This discussion guide

- ❖ May be used solo, in partners, or with a small group;
- ❖ May be completed in full or simply cherry-picked and sampled (i.e., you do *not* have to answer all of the questions, just the ones that resonate with you);
- ❖ Is not necessarily intended to be a simple, straight-through book-study guide for a group (e.g., chapter lengths and question numbers vary; one meeting could potentially be spent on just one or two questions; some questions are basic, while others invite you to the next level; in essence, the intention is to offer aids for discussion that a group can adapt to its individual needs);
- ❖ Should aid in working through and deepening one's understanding of the content of the book *Bandersnatch*;
- ❖ May help one understand one's own creative process and collaborative needs;
- ❖ May be useful in strengthening collaborative group relationships of all types.

Chapter 1
Dusting for Fingerprints

1.   Most of us have a clear gut response, either positive or negative, when we hear the term "group work." Write about or discuss your past experiences with working in groups.

2.   Have you ever seen a collaborative effort through to a successful end? What made it work so well? Have you ever participated in what turned out to be a disastrous collaborative task? Where did it go awry?

         Think about and describe your previous experience with successful collaborative efforts. You can either write about these or discuss them with your partner or group.

3.   In DOING WHAT THEY DID, Diana Glyer notes that "creativity is a messy business." Take some time to write about or discuss your own "untidy" creative process. Here are a few questions that may help you: How do you ordinarily go about creating and improving something? How has your process changed or grown over time?

4.   Think back to a project or piece you created a draft of, received feedback on, and then revised in some fashion. If you have those drafts available to you, take a look at them. If you don't have them available, comb your memory and consider how the drafts changed after external feedback.

         Take some time to write about or discuss how your project did (or did *not*) change for the better after you gained some outside perspective on it.

Chapter 2
"An Unexpected Party"

1.   The Inklings were hardly the first, or the last, collaborative group focused on literary
       conversation, writing, and art-making. Others that come easily to mind include the
       following:
       - The English Romantic poets (Wordsworth, Coleridge, Keats, etc.) in England and
         particular the Lake District
       - The Bloomsbury group (Virginia Woolf, John Maynard Keynes, E.M. Forster,
         Lytton Strachey, etc.) in London
       - The Algonquin Round Table (Dorothy Parker, George S. Kaufman, Harpo Marx,
         etc.) in New York City
       - The Factory (Andy Warhol, Truman Capote, Bob Dylan, Salvador Dali, etc.) in New
         York City
       - Stratford-on-Odeon (Hemingway, James Joyce, Gertrude Stein, F. Scott Fitzgerald)
         in Paris
       - And even The Socrates School (Socrates, Plato, Xenophon)

       It can be instructive to read more about how other literary and writing groups structured
       themselves and operated. If this interests you, Wikipedia is a great place to begin. It may be
       also interesting to consider how different factors played roles in different groups--gender
       make-up of the group, historical time period, the political and cultural realities at work,
       location (Ancient Greece, England, the United States), etc.

2.   In this chapter, Glyer lucidly depicts how the Inklings structured their meetings. Drawing
       on this, on your research of other groups, and on your own experience in groups and
       meetings, consider what kinds of settings, routines, and structures you find appealing to you.

       Think about questions of formal and informal structures, scheduled and spontaneous
       gatherings, space for reading and discussion and constructive feedback, boisterous and
       public places or quiet and intimate locations, and the creation of what is known as

"psychological safety." What sorts of group norms do you think you would respond well to? Write about these or discuss them with your group.

3.   If you're working with a partner or group, or if you'd like to try doing so, why not schedule and try a read-and-respond (or a show-and-respond, or present-and-respond) session? This can work whether you're writing, creating visual work, making music, shooting films, or delivering performances.

Such a session can be structured in one of several ways:
   (a) Each person brings his or her own piece--you may or may not want to establish length/time limits--to read, show, or present and receive feedback on.
   (b) All persons create to the same or similar prompt--this can be done in advance or on the spot during the meeting--and then all share and receive feedback.
   (c) Can you think of other approaches that sound more appealing to you?

Chapter 3
The Heart of the Company

1. As Glyer notes in this chapter, when we feel we "may have embarked on the impossible" (30), we need resonators. Think about those who have served as resonators in your life--those who have encouraged you, bought in, believed, shown interest in you and your work, caught the vision, helped you make the leap, served as an interested audience, inspired or compelled you to produce something new, demonstrated enthusiasm for you and your work, or even just provided for small needs such as a cup of tea. Who is it that has vibrated at your frequency? Write about or discuss them here. How did they serve as resonators for you?

    Have you ever served as a resonator for someone else? Write or discuss that experience from the other side.

2. How do you respond:
    -to praise?
    -to pressure, pushing, and persuasion?
    -to calls for perseverance?
    -to procrastination?
    -to perfectionism?

3. What forms of "nagging" work for you, if any?

4. Write about or discuss the differences between "atta-girl-ing" and "atta-boy-ing" versus the kind of praise that seems to be "inner health made audible" (31). What makes for good and useful praise?

5.   What "sparks" have inspired you to begin various projects? What "sparks" have incited you to complete projects? Write about these or discuss them with your group.

6.   On pp. 40-41, Diana Glyer discusses that, while many writers and artists derive their ideas from "deep wells of personal inspiration," others seek ideas and receive motivation from external sources. Write about or discuss the question of from whence your ideas come.

7.   In the same section, Glyer relates instances in which members of the Inklings suggested story ideas for one another. These ideas were met with responses of "Well, why not?" and "I might."

Here's a thought: Consider the possibility of this exercise with your partner or group. Whether you're new to one another or the oldest of friends, whether you've worked together since the Middle Ages or are just embarking on this activity of collaboration, this could work. Try a suggestion blitz, a freeflowing brainstorm of ideas *for each other* to consider pursuing in whatever particular art form may be one's own. The ideas can be crazy or epic, and no one is obligated to take anyone else's suggestion...but who knows what could possibly come of it? After all, *why not?*

8.   In the last section of this chapter (pp. 46-49), Glyer explores the Inklings' support for one another even *after* the work was completed and published. They bought, shared, gave, promoted, lent, recommended, and even reviewed one another's stories and books.

Take a few minutes to reread that section, if it is not fresh in your mind. You'll find in the explanation and examples that the Inklings' reviews provided compliments, encouragement, generous praise, unabashed enthusiasm, *specific* admiration, occasional gentle teasing (in cases where the authors knew one another well), and they demonstrated deep familiarity with the text. As Glyer makes clear, one brings one's careful and honest best to the writing of a review for a friend.

As a final possibly activity for this chapter, consider one of the following:
- Write a letter in which you praise a writer you've read for his/her good work.
- Write a review for a book you have read, and post it on Amazon or Goodreads (or both). If the work is in another medium, consider writing a review that you publish on your blog or your social media page.
- If you're working with a partner or group, consider a review exchange, an agreement to review one another's work, whether these reviews are informal (unpublished but given to the creator of the work) or formal (published in some capacity).

Chapter 4
"I've a good mind to punch you in the head."

1.   In this chapter, Diana Glyer explores the necessary counterpart to praise and encouragement--criticism. Speaking in terms of "good-natured conflict" and "the power of opposition," she notes the proper conditions for this sort of criticism to be effective: "honest critique," delivered with "healthy respect," and received with gratitude (53-57).

      How well do you take criticism or opposition? Historically? Currently? Write about this or discuss it with your group.

2.   The proverb notes that as iron sharpens iron, so, too, a person sharpens his friend (Proverbs 27:17). The Inklings weren't in it to receive a mere "butter bath," but rather to provide "real, substantial critique," hungering as they did for "rational opposition" (55, 53).

      Who has been your iron? Who, through conflict and friction, has sharpened you? Who has been good for your mind? How and why? Write about them or discuss them with your group.

3.   One key to maintaining a healthy balance seems to be to ensure the critique is not personal (56). The critique-provider does not claim a conclusive argument (56). The end goal is not to win an argument but to exchange, listen, disagree, adjust, modify, stretch, and learn (57).

      When your friends don't like your work (or aspects of it), how can you keep it from being personal? As a creator, what can you do to separate yourself from your work so that you can receive the critique thoughtfully and with gratitude? As a critique-provider, what can you do to "point out shortcomings and suggest new directions for the work" without making it about creator of the work? How do you distinguish between correction and condemnation? Write about these questions or discuss them with your group.

4.   Whom do you listen to? How do you decide whom you'll listen and whose feedback you'll disregard? How do you separate good critique from personal bias and quirk? How do you prevent jealousy--in yourself? in others? Explore these questions in writing and discuss them with your group.

5.   One possible way to practice giving and receiving opposition in a spirit of exchange might be to use a different issue as a starting point and to engage in an essay exchange, as Lewis and Barfield did across a nine-year stretch (56-7).

The word "essay" was a originally verb that meant "to attempt or try." Thus, an essay is an attempt, an effort, a trial, an experiment that tests the quality of an idea or claim.

To practice impersonal opposition, why not pick an idea--anything from points of theology or history to celebrity news or current politics may serve as a source for such an idea--and write an essay in which you "try on" and explore a position on that idea? Your partner or group members may do the same, about different ideas and positions.

Once the essays are complete, exchange them with other group members. After carefully reading and considering their position, write a response essay in which you seek to point the shortcomings, dispute issues of logic, articulate points of contention using "extremely precise" language, quote from and refer other thinkers and writers on the subject (56).

The key is to remember that (a) your issue is with the idea, not the writer of the idea; and (b) this is an exercise for stretching and growth, not for crushing victory. (Reread Glyer's description of the "Great War" on pages 56-57 for a refresher on the attitude in which Lewis and Barfield wrote and exchanged their essay-letters.) As William Blake said, "Opposition is true friendship." Perhaps this impersonal but no less impassioned practice will deepen the friendship enough to prepare you for the next step: providing measured critique of one another's own original work.

6.   In DOING WHAT THEY DID, Diana Glyer summarizes the two features of strong creative groups: passionate interest in similar things *and* diversity of personalities and points of view. She notes the first is the group glue and the second is necessary for perspective and breadth.

It may be useful and instructive to have some conversation around passions--though if you're in a creative group together, it might be logical to conclude that you already have some ideas about this--and around personality types. Whether you use the Myers-Briggs, Enneagram, StrengthsFinders, Love Languages, or any other indicator of personality and work style isn't the issue; the issue is understanding the breadth of personalities within your group and having a clear sense of the strengths and needs each member brings. (The Myers-Briggs test, the MBTI Instrument, may be accessed for free online, as may other inventories and tests.)

Chapter 5
"Drat that Omnibus!"

1.   As Glyer notes right out of the gate in this chapter, "writers who read each other's work" engage in **praise**, **critique**, and even "very, very specific recommendations" that we tend to call **editing** feedback--no small duties and responsibilities.

Furthermore, she chalks up the Inklings' effectiveness to (as Anne Gere called it) their "textual indeterminacy"--that is, "the writer's ability to stay open to the possibility of substantial change." (74) Indeed, collaboration requires openness and vulnerability.

How do we, then, stay open, with our work, our egos, our feelings on the line? How do we live up to the great responsibilities we bear to one another in our groups? Whether you believe in the God of Lewis and Tolkien, share in the Greeks' habit of invoking the appropriate Muse before beginning work, or simply acknowledge that a little mindfulness at the outset of an effort or a meeting can be a good thing, adopting a focusing blessing, prayer, invocation, or declaration of your agreed-upon goals might be a nice way to begin your work times together.

Consider creating together a collective opening of your own. Or you could ask each group member to create an original brief opener. Or each member could write an opener, and then a new corporate one made by weaving together a line from each member's creation. Regardless of your approach, it can't hurt to remind all members present of our higher purposes and positive intentions.

2.   Allowing for differences in process--The Inklings didn't try to change each other. Tolkien's personality included a tendency to write a very many drafts and reworkings of his books. "And the Inklings reinforces rather than restrained this natural tendency" (76).

How do we reinforce our fellow creatives' natural tendencies? If, in previous chapters, you have considered and discussed your own creative processes, this might be a good time to revisit those, or to explore, in writing and/or discussion, how each group member likes to receive feedback, where each group member tends to get stuck, what has worked historically for each group member to become unstuck, whether one creates (like Tolkien) "in fits and starts" or abandons the project in favor of other temporary pursuits, etc.

3. Something to try: Write someone's feedback in the form of a conversation among 3 (or more) people. Perhaps, as Lewis did it, the conversants could be a series of scholarly or popular "experts" (84). The practice may have a distancing and even entertaining effect, removing what could be potentially be the sting of difficult criticism. Consider providing thorough feedback on the three levels Tolkien engaged in with Lewis: the level of the whole text, the level of the sentence, and the level of the word (96). (What would the three levels, from global to precise, be in *your* art form?)

4. If your group is searching for exercises in revision, members could do worse than to emulate Lewis and Tolkien, trying on their revision methods for size.

As Glyer notes, Tolkien "wrote things out in order to discover what he wanted to say (89). Tolkien also incorporated a large majority (though not all) of Lewis's feedback and suggestions, writing multiple revision drafts and bringing them back for further commentary.

Lewis, on the other hand, worked out his ideas in his head, sometimes over years, and then wrote quickly and produced seemingly complete drafts, but he remained open to changing what he wrote (90), regularly requesting feedback (91). As Glyer explains, Lewis often tried out his story ideas in more than one form (different poem types, plays, lectures, radio talks, stories, novels). Lewis also tweaked and refined small details and inconsistencies.

Group members in search of stretching could try drafting or revising their work differently than they are regularly accustomed to do. Options could include:
- Generate multiple drafts or versions, incorporating received feedback into each.
- Consult group members for feedback on the idea before it's even realized in draft form, then create the draft.
- Radically revise a draft at the core concept level, based on commentary received.
- Explore the concept in an entirely different genre or form or mood/tone.
- Experiment with an interactive writing process that seeks input from a variety of reliable person, even those outside the group.
- Incorporate or address feedback, others' objections, and even mindful rejection of suggestions quite overtly in your revised draft (a la Lewis, 95).

5.   In DOING WHAT THEY DID, Glyer suggests that asking for feedback early in the creative process can make a huge difference. Consider these possible exercises:
- Propose a story or book idea and workshop it with your group before drafting it. (This could be an enlightening exercise regardless of your art form--song idea, film idea, idea for a painting or sculpture....)
- Brainstorm ideas *without originators' names*. Make notes about the ensuing discussion, also without names.

Chapter 6
Mystical Caboodle

1.   In this chapter, Glyer explores the definitions and tolerances of what counts as "collaboration." The minimum definition, she notes, is that it is "two or more individuals who think up a project and then work on it together from start to finish" (103). In the example of the Lewis brothers, the early collaboration was prompted by change, successfully blended independent visions into a cohesive whole, and required time.

In point of fact, collaboration can be as formal as some of the Inklings meetings and as informal as two brothers world-building in an attic.

Take some time to brainstorm a comprehensive list of collaborations you've engaged in, both formal and informal. You may have considered, in earlier chapters, some of your collaborations, but this chapter may have broadened your understanding of what collaboration encompasses.

2.   If you noted nothing else in this chapter, we hope you spotted the evidence that collaboration can actually be a lot of fun! Author Madeleine L'Engle, in *Walking on Water*, an exploration of faith and art, talks about watching the child who is "seriously" at play and notes that work and play are easy to confuse in that setting, concluding from it that "our work should be our play" (L'Engle 167). Similarly, Julia Cameron writes in *The Artist's Way*, that "serious art is born from serious play" (Cameron, Week 6).

In the spirit of play, and particularly in the spirit of the play the members of the Inklings engaged in as they transformed challenges into play, consider participating with your collaboration partner or group in some of the games they devised:
- Write a collaborative poem, turning hardships into satirical humor, changing names based on the features of the "characters." (See p. 106)
- Engage in a story round-robin. (See p. 106)
- Do a poetry hand-off, or write a serial poem together. (In a form? In free verse?) (See p. 106)

- Play with a rhyming competition. (See p. 107)
- Write something abcedarian. (A poem? An encyclopedia of something?) Pick a topic and be exhaustive. (See p. 108)
- Devise a mock test for each other. (See pp. 109-10)
- Dare we suggest a walking tour? Where will you always stop? (See pp. 108-10)

3.   Or, on a more serious note:
- Consider a joint project in which you collaborate on a particular section, based on the expertise in the group. (See pp. 112-13)
- Consider creating a collection to honor a friend or as a gift to someone or for a cause. (See. p. 113)
- Consider writing or recording a commentary on one of your friend's or group member's projects (or trading commentary for commentary). (See p. 114)
- While it is important for a writer to read her own work aloud in her own voice, it can also be instructive to hear someone else read it. Thus, consider the possibility of having your own work read back to you by another fluent reader. (See p. 116)
- Consider creating a map of your own, or of another group member's, work. (Consider the possibilities even if the work is not narrative, even if the work is not written.) (See p. 116)

4.   If your group or partnership has been working together collaboratively for an extended period, it could be time to consider whether you are in the "'collective action' stage," in which some of your corporate attention and energies shift outward, a stage in which "members decide to carry out a group project aimed at winning support for their vision outside their own network" (119).

As Glyer notes, the Inklings mostly kept their outside activity to publicizing each others' work, but they did occasionally work for political change based on principle and collective convictions (119-20).

It may not be a planned effort on the part of your group, but instead a response to an immediate need or situation. In any case, is your collaborative circle willing to countenance the discussion? It may be worth conversing about.

5.   At the close of the chapter comes an exquisite, if brief, consideration of the nature of collaborative friendship (121-22). Lewis, in *The Four Loves*, draws distinctions between working face to face and side by side. He declares that one finds true

warriors/poets/philosophers/Christians by working beside and with them rather than by staring them in the eye.

Take some time to write about and discuss both your experiences and the implications of this distinction.

Chapter 7
Faces in a Mirror

1. The Inklings were constantly writing about each other (125). Some instances were technical exercises; others were clever, comical poems; still others were characters in novels and stories (131).

    Consider, in the spirit of both play and deepening friendship, the possibility of creating lighthearted works about and/or including your group members. For example, the group members could write clerihews about one another, in which one could explore one's respect for and levels of knowledge about one's friends (128-9).

2. The Inklings also wrote serious works about each other: Lewis's poem about Charles Williams about the world after Williams died, Tolkien's reflective poem about Williams, or Owen Barfield's and others' obituaries of Lewis. These are generally not mere idealizations but balanced--frank and also warm, appreciative of the deep differences that elevated the friendship rather than damaging it.

    Furthermore, the chapter title is not accidental. The Inklings served as faces in a mirror in the sense that members were seen and known by the gathering of friends-slash-collaborators.

3. Tolkien believed that that "human creativity is a reflection of the Divine," a notion called "sub-creation" (130). What are your beliefs and convictions about creation and creativity? Explore them in writing and consider discussing them with your group.

4. At the risk of sounding macabre, we could also suggest an optional activity of writing not-yet-dead obituaries for one another in your group. All too often, we do not say what we'd like to say to or about others until they've passed out of this world. Wouldn't it be an interesting exercise to obituarize or eulogize our friends and collaborators now, while they

can still hear it? Consider this: In what ways would you not be you without your particular creative companions?

5.   In DOING WHAT THEY DID, Glyer states that "the insights we gain from one another become part of the fabric of our own work" (145). Whose insights have influenced and woven their way into your work? How? Can you trace the threads to their origins?

Chapter 8
Leaf-Mould and Memories

1.   In this chapter, Glyer takes issue with the romantic but unfounded notion of the "lone-genius idea" (as Joshua Wolf Shenk called it), listing a number of famous examples of creative collaboration aside from the Inklings as support (148-9). Glyer uses an apt metaphor: "...normal creativity starts to look a lot less like a lone genius struck with a single breathtaking insight and whole lot more like a series of sparks coming from different directions, each spark inspiring something new" (149).

She goes on to allay some "yeah, buts." This does not render invalid the ideas of individual talent, work to master one's craft, or reflection hours of solitude. The fact is, Glyer asserts, we need both the "bold individual" *and* the "collaborative collective." (149)

In essence, what Glyer suggests in this chapter is that these two seemingly opposing ideas are a beautiful paradox, that they can and must exist in constant creative tension. Charles Williams's solitude and companionship must balance out one another (150). Randy Komisar's "efficiency thinking" and "relational thinking" must coexist and pull against each other (150).

What are some other creative tensions that (co)exist in your particular art form or creative process? Consider doing some thinking, writing, and/or discussion around these ideas of paradox and creative tension.

2.   Karen Burke LeFevre's analogy of the small trees in a tall forest is instructive (see p. 151). John Donne's (at least partly) famous assertion comes to mind: "No man is an island entire of itself; every man / is a piece of the continent, a part of the main...." So, too, does the widely quoted wisdom of personal success luminary Jim Rohn: "You are the average of the five people you spend the most time with."

● Have you taken time to consider the forest you've planted yourself in?
● Do you need a transplant?

- Have you given thought to the continent of which you are a piece? (See Donne quote.)
- Have you broken off?
- Have you examined your own law of average?
- What does it look like and are you satisfied with it?

Consider some or all of these questions in writing and possibly in discussion with your partner or group.

3. This might be an interesting point in the text to consider issues of introversion and extroversion. As Glyer notes, the balance between alone time and time together will differ for each person (150).

   What are your ideal proportions of solitude and company, of silence and social interaction? How have your needs changed over time? From project to project? From season to season?

4. In the section on widening circles, Glyer invokes the Great Conversation that has been in progress for millennia (and perhaps even outside of time). If you read this brief section quickly, please consider rereading it (or even the whole beautiful chapter) while savoring it (see pp. 152-4).

   Some of the best written works we read, music we listen to, art pieces we view, or films we watch today are works in conversation with other antecedent or contemporary works. Sometimes this conversation comes out of influence; other times it's intentional direct response to another work. No art occurs in a vacuum. Tolkien and Neil Gaiman alike allude to the "leaf-mould" or the compost that myths and fairy tales and the historical swath of stories provide for our seedling ideas.

   Consider--in writing, in discussion--the notions of conversation, exchange, interdependence, and "powerful play" (155-8).
   - What is your take on the idea of interdependence--a suggestion that many, such as Karen Burke LeFevre, Charles Williams, and Madeleine L'Engle support--the idea that there is no life "that does not owe itself to the life and labor of someone else" (157)?
   - Whom do you see yourself to be in conversation with?
   - Whom would you *like* to be in conversation with?
   - Which stories and predecessors and contemporaries do you consider to be your "leaf-mould," your compost?
   - Which of your "inventive acts" have been "*made possible* by other people"? (156)

● And who is it you might be saving your own last pages for (159)? Who are you hoping will converse with you?

Epilogue
Doing What the Inklings Did

If you're sold on the idea of collaboration and its necessary role in the creative process, this Epilogue provides you with some practical steps for emulating the successful practices of the Inklings. Rather than belabor what is already a very clear and actionable series of steps, we will simply ask a few leading questions that we hope will help you move forward on your goals as early as today.

1. **Start Small**: Can you name one person you would be interested in speaking to about starting a creative collaborative group with? Write down that person's name and consider how you will present your hopeful vision. Write an appointment on the calendar for talking to this person.

2. **Stay Focused**: Discuss and select a single defining purpose. If you try to do too many things at first, the group may never get off the ground. Craig McKeown, in his book *Essentialism*, helpfully reminds readers that "priority" is a singular word, and a plural form of it did not exist until the early twentieth century! Discuss and identify your group's singular priority and make it work for a while before adding anything else.

3. **Meet Often**: Determine a regular calendar and stick to it. Make it frequent enough to make it effective. Other contact and connections can branch out from there.

4. **Embrace Difference**: Remember that Inklings did not try to change each other's creative approach or personalities. Instead they worked within the differences and appreciated the friendships that resulted from them. (Could any two writers/men be more different than Tolkien and Lewis in their creative processes?) As you grow to recognize your differences, note them and celebrate them. The proverb says, "As iron sharpens iron, so one person sharpens another," and this effect does not occur without edges and angles, opposition and

friction. Glyer includes the key: "Learn to listen generously, especially when you disagree" (164). How will you go about learning this vital skill? What are some things you might do to practice the appreciation of difference?

5. **Start Early and Intervene Often**: Remember that input and assistance can occur anywhere along the draft process--before, during, and after. Whether it's just a crazy idea someone had in the shower this morning or an essentially completed manuscript or even a published work, collaborative contributions are still valuable. Are you open to feedback at any point along your creative process? Can you see how you might provide helpful input even when a work is "done"?

6. **Criticize but Don't Silence**: As Glyer clearly asserts, "Correction is necessary…[but] it is one thing to criticize; it is quite another to dismiss someone's work altogether" (165). A group can weather "I don't personally like this," but "This isn't any good" will certainly have a corrosive effect on everyone involved (165). Social science has terms for this distinction: "psychological safety" and "psychological danger." Can you recognize the difference between personal opinion and the overall value of a work? Can you openly discuss when someone in the group is feeling psychologically unsafe? How will you work that openness into your group norms?

7. **Vary Feedback**: Practice giving different types of feedback at different times; expand your repertoire. Glyer provides a useful list here of types of responses one might provide, and readers can revisit Chapters 2, 3, and 4 for another look at ways to give thoughtful commentary, and critique that is experienced by all parties as being rooted in positive intentions. How will you break past the old-school notion that giving feedback means to tell someone what's wrong and how to fix it? How might you mindfully practice broadening your feedback skills?

8. **Increase the Channels**: We live in amazing times, with magnificent technologies available to us. You don't have to let proximity or distance determine your group composition or meeting abilities. Would you consider brainstorming a list of available means of communication and modes of idea exchange, and discuss those with your group in order to expand your collective capabilities?

9.   **Try More Than One**: It's not infidelity. It's cross-pollination. One size rarely fits all, and one collaborative arrangement is not likely to fill all of your needs and desired purposes. Have you considered what other types of groups or structures might benefit you?

10.   **Think Outside the Group**: Your familiar, trusted group provides a psychologically safe place for you take risks in sharing your ideas and creations. It can be a place to practice and be emboldened to go outside of the group and into other venues and situations to share your work. Glyer list should provoke some good ideas (168). Which of her suggested ventures would you potentially consider? What other ideas come to mind?

11.   **Taking First Steps**: If the rest of the points in this epilogue are overwhelming or feel as though they might apply a little further on in the future but not right now, Glyer includes a simple trio of suggestions to get you started in a smaller scale. They include **reading**, **internet** (online participation) and a **dyad** (the power of two, just talking with one other person).

Are these approachable activities for you? Can you take these first three steps?
    1.   Have you identified a book about collaboration and creativity that you might be interested in reading first?
    2.   Have you explored and selected an online community that you could see yourself joining?
    3.   Have you named one person you might ask to start this conversation with?

Do you want to grow? Are you game? Do you feel like influencing a bandersnatch today?

◻ ◻ ◻